How to Use This Book

The **Teaching Versions** of *Elements of Reading: Fluency* will help you guide children to become fluent readers. Because fluency is not an isolated skill but is closely linked to word knowledge and comprehension, each **Teaching Version** contains the following types of teacher support:

■ **Fluency teaching suggestions** to help children become proficient in reading with expression (prosody).

■ **Word knowledge teaching suggestions** to build children's proficiency in reading words and understanding their structure and meanings. The word knowledge suggestions address recognition of high-frequency words, decoding skills, structural analysis skills, and knowledge of word meanings.

■ **S**e **qu**e **...** literal comprehension at the sentence level.

■ **Text comprehension questions** to help children develop inferential comprehension. Additional comprehension questions are provided in the **Teacher's Lesson Folder**.

After children have completed the repeated reading activities outlined on page 4.8 of the **Teacher's Lesson Folder**, use the reduced **Student Book** pages and teaching suggestions in this **Teaching Version** to provide explicit page-by-page instruction.

Day and Night

■ **Fluency Focus**

Punctuation: Using correct intonation for questions

Punctuation: Observing junctures indicated by commas

Text Format: Reading headings

■ **Word Knowledge Focus**

Structural Analysis Plurals with -*s*

High-Frequency Words (Boldface words appear in each book of the theme.)

and, are, at, black, blue, can, close, **day**, do, from, full, get, go, home, in, is, it, light, most, **night**, of, on, open, people, play, run, **see**, **sleep**, some, the, their, **they**, to, up, we, what, you, your

■ **Sentence Comprehension Focus**

Comprehending stated comparisons and contrasts

■ **Text Comprehension Focus**

Drawing conclusions

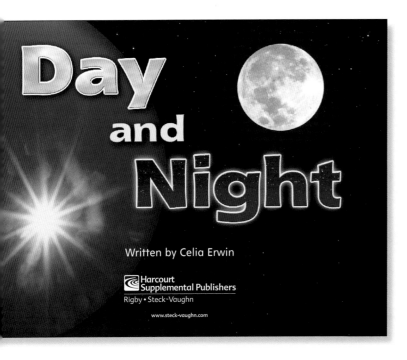

Getting Started

To begin, read the title page aloud or invite a volunteer to do so.

Book Summary

This nonfiction book explores how day and night are different. Various topics such as the sky, flowers, and towns present a series of stated contrasts.

■ Fluency

Point out the comma after the introductory phrase "In the day." Explain that the comma signals that the reader should pause slightly before going on with the rest of the sentence. Model reading the sentence without the pause and with it. Ask children which reading has the pause after "In the day." Have children read the sentence in unison

■ Word Knowledge

Write the theme high-frequency words *day*, *night*, *see*, *sleep*, and *they* on chart paper. Invite children to read them aloud with you. Then ask children which of the words appears on page 2.

In the day, the sun shines.
It is light outside.

2

■ Sentence Comprehension

Ask   *What shines in the day?* (the sun)

At night, the moon shines.
It is dark outside.

3

Point out the comma after the introductory phrase "At night." Invite a
volunteer to read the sentence correctly.
Be sure the volunteer pauses slightly at
the comma. Encourage children to look
for commas after other introductory
phrases as they move through the book.

■ Word Knowledge

Direct children's attention to the list of
theme high-frequency words on chart
paper. Ask children to identify the
high-frequency word on page 3.

■ Sentence Comprehension

Ask   *These two pages tell two ways that day and
night are different. What are the two ways?*
(In the day, the sun shines; at night, the
moon shines. In the day it is light outside; at
night, it is dark outside.)

3

■ Fluency

Direct children's attention to the heading "Sky." Guide children in recalling that headings should be followed by a pause.

Point out the comma in the first sentence and ask children what it tells a reader (to pause slightly).

■ Word Knowledge

Have children refer to the list of theme high-fequency words on chart paper. Have children identify the one on the page.

Sky

On most days, the sky is blue.
We can see clouds in the sky.

4

At night, the sky is black.
We can see stars in the sky.

5

■ Fluency

Point out the comma in the first sentence. Ask what the comma signals (pause). Invite a volunteer to read the page aloud.

■ Word Knowledge

Direct children's attention to "clouds" on page 4 and read the word aloud. Point out the *s* at the end of the word. Explain that adding *s* to *cloud* forms a plural, or more than one. Ask children to find the other two plurals on pages 4–5 ("days," "stars").

■ Sentence Comprehension

Ask *How is the color of the sky different in the day and at night?* (blue most days, black at night)

■ Fluency

As you read the second sentence on this page, make sure you say the word "some" with a little more force. Ask children how this force helps a listener. Guide children to recognize that slightly emphasizing the word helps a listener quickly understand that not all open in the light.

Review with children all the places they should pause when they read page 6: after "Flowers, "In the day," and after each sentence.

■ Word Knowledge

Remind children that *s* at the end of some words signals that the word means more than one. Ask children to find the plural word on the page (*flowers*).

Flowers

In the day, flowers get light from the sun. Some flowers open in the light.

6

At night, some flowers close up.
They stay closed in the dark.

7

■ Sentence Comprehension

Ask *How are some flowers different in the day and at night?* (Some open in the day and close at night.)

■ Fluency

As you read the first sentence on this page, make sure you say the word "some" with a little more force. Ask children how this force helps a listener. Guide children to recognize that slightly emphasizing the word helps a listener quickly understand that not all flowers close up.

■ Word Knowledge

Direct children's attention to the theme high-frequency word *They*. Explain that *they* stands for people or things already mentioned. Ask children what *they* stands for here (the flowers that close up). Have children find the other theme high-frequency word on the page.

■ Fluency

Point out the comma after "In the day." Ask what the comma tells the reader to do (pause). Invite children to read the page together.

■ Word Knowledge

Direct children's attention to "birds" and "wings." Point out the *s* at the end of each word. Ask if the words mean one or more than one. Have children find the theme high-frequency words on the page.

Birds

In the day, most birds are awake. They open their wings in the sun.

8

At night, most birds go to sleep.
They close their eyes in the dark.

9

Fluency

Read the first sentence without a pause after "At night." Ask children whether you read the sentence well. Elicit a good reading (one with a pause after the phrase) from volunteers.

Word Knowledge

Direct children's attention to the list of high-frequency words on chart paper and ask them to find the list words on the page.

Sentence Comprehension

Ask *In what way are most birds different during the day and night?* (They are awake in the day and asleep at night.)

Write *dog* on the board paper. Ask children to find the word on the page that means "more than one dog" ("dogs"). Have children say *dog* and *dogs*.

Dogs

In the day, most dogs are awake. They run and play in the sun.

10

At night, most dogs go to sleep.
They close their eyes in the dark.

11

Review with children all the places they should pause on pages 10–11. Lead children in a fluent reading of the two pages. Make sure children pause after the heading and after the commas.

■ Sentence Comprehension

Ask *Dogs do different things in the day and at night. What are those things?* (They run and play in the sun; they close their eyes in the dark.)

As you read the page aloud, stop after each pause and ask children to explain why you paused there.

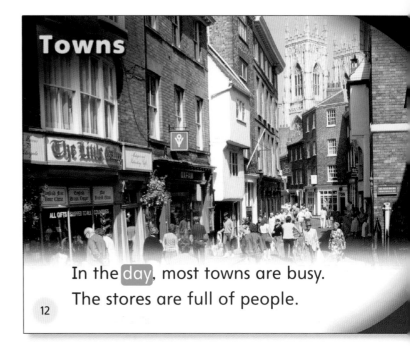

Towns

In the day, most towns are busy.
The stores are full of people.

12

■ **Sentence Comprehension**

Ask   *What makes most towns busy in the day?*
(The stores are full of people.)

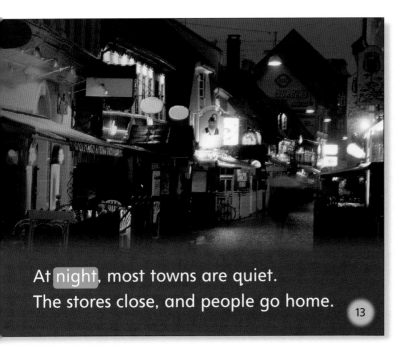

At night, most towns are quiet.
The stores close, and people go home.

13

■ **Fluency**

Point out the comma in the second sentence and the pause it signals. Invite children to read along with you in a choral reading of the page.

■ **Word Knowledge**

Ask children to find the word on pages 12–13 that has *s* at the end and means "more than one town" ("towns"). Then have children find the word that is the plural of *store* ("stores").

■ **Sentence Comprehension**

Ask   *What are towns like at night?* (quiet; stores are closed, and people go home)

■ Fluency

Point out that unlike the sentences that have come before, the sentences on page 14 end with question marks instead of periods. Remind children that a reader's voice should go up at the end of a question. Invite volunteers to read the page aloud.

You

What do you do in the day?
Do you run and play in the sun?

14

What do you do at night?
Do you close your eyes and go to sleep?

15

■ **Fluency**

Invite children to read page 15 along with you. Make sure children pause appropriately and read the questions with appropriate intonation.

■ **Word Knowledge**

Refer children to the list of theme high-frequency words on chart paper. Have them identify the words on pages 14–15.

15

Explain the purpose of an index—to tell a reader where to find information about topics in the book.

Point out that when we read nonfiction books aloud, we do not read the index. Model how to use an index, asking questions such as *Where can I find information about dogs?*

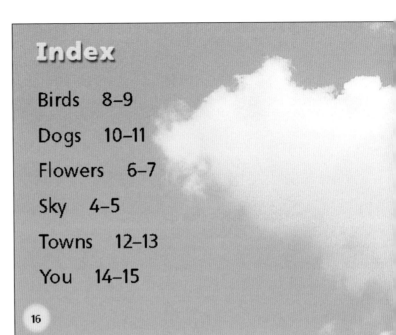

Index

Birds   8–9

Dogs   10–11

Flowers   6–7

Sky   4–5

Towns   12–13

You   14–15

16

■ Text Comprehension

Ask *Why is it light during the day?* (The sun is shining where we are.)

Ask *Why is it dark at night?* (The sun is not shining where we are.)

Ask *How are stores different in the day and at night?* (They are full of people in the day.)

Ask *How are you different in the day and at night?* (awake and busy in the day; asleep at night)

■ Fluency Flip Page

The **Fluency Flip Page** of the **Student Book** contains a passage from the book to facilitate timed reading. For more information on timed reading and other ways of assessing fluency, see the **Teacher's Lesson Folder**.

Dogs

In the day, most dogs are awake. 1

They run and play in the sun. 8

At night, most dogs go to sleep. 15

They close their eyes in the dark. 22

Towns 29

In the day, most towns are busy. 30

The stores are full of people. 37

At night, most towns are quiet. 43

The stores close, and people go home. 49

You 56

What do you do in the day? 57

Do you run and play in the sun? 64

What do you do at night? 72

Do you close your eyes and go to sleep? 78